hrjc

TULSA CITY-COUNTY LIBRARY

D0850039

COOL
PAPER ART

KIRIGAMI
PAPER CUTTING AND FOLDING

RACHAEL L.
THOMAS

Checkerboard Library

An Imprint of Abdo Publishing
abdobooks.com

abdobooks.com

Published by Abdo Publishing, a division of ABDO, PO Box 398166, Minneapolis, Minnesota 55439. Copyright © 2020 by Abdo Consulting Group, Inc. International copyrights reserved in all countries. No part of this book may be reproduced in any form without written permission from the publisher. Checkerboard Library™ is a trademark and logo of Abdo Publishing.

Printed in the United States of America, North Mankato, Minnesota
052019
092019

THIS BOOK CONTAINS
RECYCLED MATERIALS

Design: Christa Schneider, Mighty Media, Inc.
Production: Mighty Media, Inc.
Editor: Liz Salzmann
Cover Photographs: Mighty Media, Inc.
Interior Photographs: iStockphoto, p. 29; Mighty Media, Inc., pp. 1, 3, 4 (pattern), 6 (both), 7 (all), 8–27 (all), 28 (pattern), 30, 31, 32; Shutterstock Images, pp. 4–5, 5, 28 (snowflakes)

The following manufacturers/names appearing in this book are trademarks: Scotch®, Westcott®

Library of Congress Control Number: 2018966249

Publisher's Cataloging-in-Publication Data
Names: Thomas, Rachael L., author.
Title: Kirigami: paper cutting and folding / by Rachael L. Thomas
Other title: Paper cutting and folding
Description: Minneapolis, Minnesota : Abdo Publishing, 2020 | Series: Cool paper art | Includes online resources and index.
Identifiers: ISBN 9781532119453 (lib. bdg.) | ISBN 9781532173912 (ebook)
Subjects: LCSH: Paper art--Juvenile literature. | Origami--Juvenile literature. | Japanese paper folding--Juvenile literature. | Paper folding (Handicraft)--Juvenile literature.
Classification: DDC 736.982--dc23

CONTENTS

KIRIGAMI

Kirigami is a form of paper art. The word comes from the Japanese words *kiru*, meaning "cut," and *gami*, meaning "paper." Kirigami artists fold and cut paper into amazing pieces of art. One of the most important elements of kirigami is **symmetry**. Artists unfold their paper to reveal perfectly symmetrical designs.

It is possible that long ago, kirigami was used in Japanese temples as a way to make offerings to the gods. Today, kirigami is often seen in Japan as part of **Buddhist** festivals. However, kirigami has become popular around the world. Anyone can be a kirigami master, including you!

MATERIALS

All you need to practice kirigami is paper and a pair of scissors. However, the kind of paper that you use can be very important, depending on the project.

Some kirigami designs require sturdy paper, such as construction paper, so that folds stay firmly in place. Other projects require cutting through several layers of paper. So, using thinner paper can make this task easier.

There are also certain household materials that are well suited to kirigami. Kitchen papers such as parchment paper, wax paper, or freezer paper are all very thin. They also come in long sheets that can be cut to any size. Be sure to ask for **permission** before using these types of paper for kirigami projects.

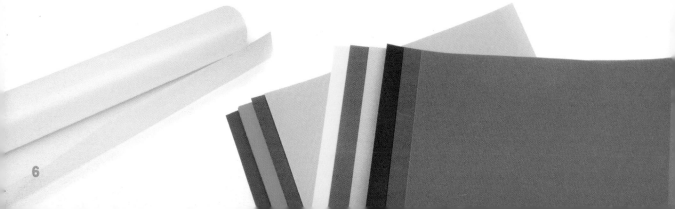

ADDITIONAL SUPPLIES

ruler

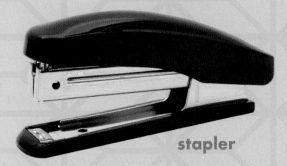

stapler

pencil

tape

scissors

THE BASICS

Kirigami requires folding as well as cutting. The most common fold is the valley fold. Use the symbols below to help you complete the projects in this book.

valley fold
Fold the paper in front like a valley.

COMMON KIRIGAMI SYMBOLS

- - - - - - - - - -	Valley fold
————————	Crease
————————	Cut line
⤻	Turn over
↻	Rotate

After folding the paper, grab your scissors! Solid lines show where to cut. Areas that will be cut away will be colored in.

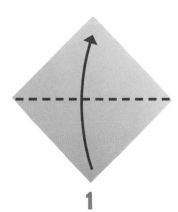

1

Place the paper on the table with a point on the top. Valley fold the bottom point to the top point.

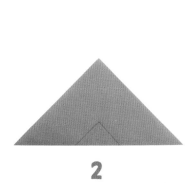

2

Draw a shape along the folded edge of the paper.

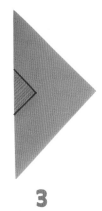

3

Color in the area you want to cut away.

4

Cut along the lines, removing the shaded area.

5

Unfold the paper to see your kirigami pattern!

CIRCLE PATTERNS

Some kirigami art forms a circular pattern. A piece of paper is folded into a wedge that has equal-size **segments**. Then patterns are cut into its edges. These patterns are repeated in each segment. When the paper is unfolded, the cuts form a circular pattern. Kirigami wedges often have eight or six segments.

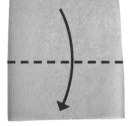

1

Place a square piece of paper on the table with a straight edge at the top. Valley fold the top edge to the bottom edge.

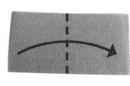

2

Valley fold the left edge to the right edge.

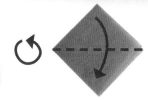

3

Rotate the paper to the left so a point is at the top. Valley fold the top point to the bottom point.

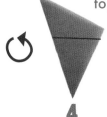

4

Rotate the paper so the long edge is on the left. Cut across the top so the sides below the cut are the same length.

5

Draw patterns on the edges. Color in the areas you want to cut away.

6

Cut along the lines.

7

Unfold the paper.

1

Place a square piece of paper on the table with a straight edge at the top. Valley fold the bottom edge to the top edge.

2

Valley fold the left edge to the right edge. Unfold.

3

Fold the bottom right corner at an angle from the center crease.

4

Fold the bottom left corner to the right edge. Cut across the top so the sides below the cut are the same length.

5

Draw patterns on the edges. Color in the areas you want to cut away.

6

Cut along the lines.

7

Unfold the paper.

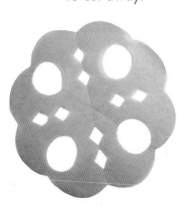

SPOOKY SPIDERWEB

- thin paper, such as wax paper
- scissors
- ruler
- pencil

1
Cut a 12-inch (30 cm) square of paper.

2
Fold the paper into a six-**segment** wedge (see page 10).

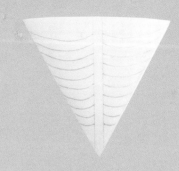

3

Draw two lines down the middle of the wedge. Mark eight or ten evenly spaced points on each line.

4

Draw curved lines from the edge to each point on the center lines.

5

Color in the areas you want to cut away. Erase the lines that cross uncolored areas.

6

Cut along the lines. Do not cut across the center lines. Unfold the paper. Hang your spooky spiderweb in a window!

PAPER DOLLS

- thin paper, such as wax paper
- scissors
- ruler
- pencil

1

Cut a 12-inch (30 cm) square of paper.

2

Fold the paper into an eight-**segment** wedge (see page 11). Rotate the wedge so it points up.

3

Draw doll shapes on the edges.
There should be half a doll on
each side. Make sure that their
arms meet in the middle.

4

Color the area outside
the doll shapes.

5

Cut along the lines.

6

Unfold the paper. You should
have a circle of eight paper dolls.

WINDOW DECORATION

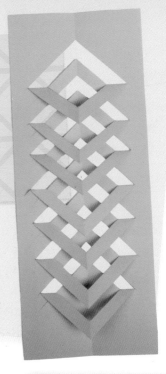

- paper
- scissors
- ruler
- pencil

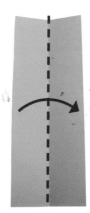

1

Cut a long rectangle out of paper. Place it on the table with a short edge at the top. Valley fold the left edge to the right edge.

2

Use a ruler to draw a vertical line near the right edge.

3

Draw a line at an angle from the fold to the vertical line.

4

Draw more angled lines under the first one. You can draw as many lines as you like. However, there must be an even number of them. Space the lines evenly.

5

Cut along each angled line. Unfold the paper.

6

The cuts should have formed V-shaped bands across the paper. Fold the bottom band down. Leave the band above it unfolded. Keep folding down every other band. Hang your paper art up on a window to see how the light shines through the pattern!

KIRIGAMI GARLAND

- colored construction paper
- scissors
- pencil
- stapler (optional)

1
Cut a piece of colored construction paper in half crosswise and lengthways to make four rectangles.

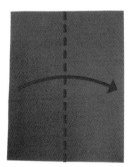

2
Place one of the rectangles on the table with a short edge at the top. Valley fold the left edge to the right edge.

3

Draw a line from the left edge to ¼ inch (0.6 cm) from the right edge. Draw a line ¼ inch (0.6 cm) below the first, but from the right edge to ¼ inch (0.6 cm) from the left edge.

4

Continue drawing lines, alternating directions. Stop when you get near the bottom of the paper.

5

Cut along the lines.
Unfold the paper.

6

Carefully pull the ends apart. For a longer **garland**, repeat steps 2 through 5 with the other paper rectangles. Staple the sections together. Then, decorate your room with your kirigami garland!

HANGING DECORATION

- 2 sheets of origami paper with different-colored sides
- ruler
- pencil
- scissors
- stapler
- braided string

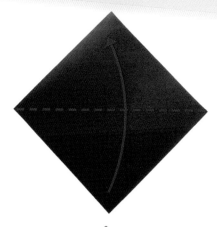

1

Place one paper square on the table with a point at the top. Valley fold the bottom point to the top point.

2

Valley fold the left point to the right point.

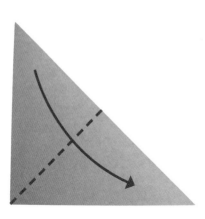

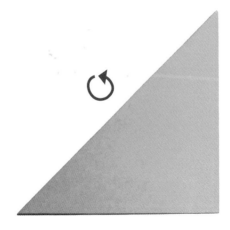

3
Valley fold the top left point
to the bottom right point.

4
Rotate the paper so the
long edge is on the left.

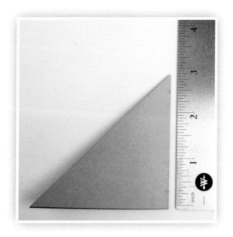

5
Make eight
evenly-spaced marks
along the right edge.

Continued on the next page.

6

Draw a horizontal line from the left edge toward the first mark. Stop about ¼ inch (0.6 cm) from the right edge. Then draw a horizontal line from the second mark to about ¼ inch (0.6 cm) from the left edge. Continue drawing lines at each mark, alternating directions.

7

Cut along the lines.

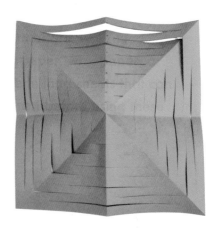

8

Carefully unfold the paper.

9

Repeat steps 1 through 8 with the second paper square.

10

Place one square on top of the other. The sides facing each other should be the same color. Staple the squares together in the middle of each edge. Thread a braided string through the cuts in the top square. Use the string to hang up your decoration.

FANCY SNOWFLAKE

- **6 sheets of white paper**
- **scissors**
- **ruler**
- **pencil**
- **clear tape**
- **stapler**

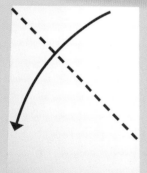

1
Place a sheet of paper on the table with a short edge at the top. Valley fold the top edge to the left edge.

2
Cut off the bottom rectangle.

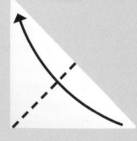

3
Fold the bottom point to the top point.

4

Turn the paper over. Place it on the table with the main fold on the bottom. Make four evenly-spaced marks along the bottom edge.

5

Draw a line from each mark that is parallel to the long edge. Cut along the lines. Stop cutting about ½ inch (1.3 cm) from the far edge.

6

Unfold the paper. Cut a small square of tape. Fold it so the sticky side faces out. Stick the tape to the underside of one of the smallest triangles.

Continued on the next page.

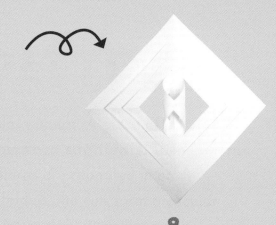

7

Bend the smallest triangles toward each other. Stick them together to form a circle.

8

Turn the paper over from side to side. Repeat steps 6 and 7 with the next-smallest triangles.

9

Repeat step 8 to stick the remaining triangles together. This is one complete snowflake unit.

10

Repeat steps 1 through 9 with the other five sheets of paper. Line the units up in two rows of three. Make sure they are all facing the same way.

11

Staple the sides of the units
in one row together.

12

Staple the bottom points of
the units together.

13

Repeat steps 11 and 12 with the
units in the second row. Then
staple the stapled points of each
set of units together.

14

Staple the last two sides
together to fully connect your
snowflake.

CONCLUSION

The art of kirigami has grown from a religious art form to something that anybody can try! As you master the basics, experiment with different designs and methods. Add decorative materials such as glitter, paint, or googly eyes to bring your kirigami to life. Shine flashlights through your kirigami pieces to cast patterned shadows on the wall.

And like a true artist, keep your eyes and ears open for inspiration. Have an adult help you find online videos of kirigami artists at work. Try some of their methods. One day, you could be the one showing your paper art to the world!

GLOSSARY

Buddhist – one who believes in the teachings of Gautama Buddha.

garland – a decorative ring or rope made of leaves, flowers, or some other material.

permission – when a person in charge says it's okay to do something.

segment – any of the parts into which a thing is divided or naturally separates.

symmetry – the property of having two halves that are the same. Something that has symmetry is symmetrical.

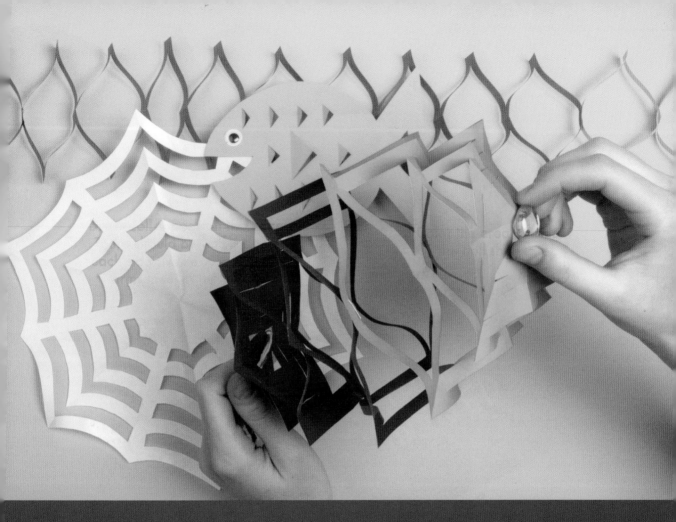

ONLINE RESOURCES

Booklinks
NONFICTION NETWORK
FREE! ONLINE NONFICTION RESOURCES

To learn more about kirigami, please visit
abdobooklinks.com or scan this QR code. These links
are routinely monitored and updated to provide the most
current information available.

INDEX